Psalm Sonnets

❧

Jane Simpson

FUTURECYCLE PRESS
www.futurecycle.org

Cover photo, "Talybont Reservoir, Brecon Beacons National Park, Powys, Wales"; author photo by Michael Schwarz; cover and interior book design by Diane Kistner; Adobe Garamond text and titling

Library of Congress Control Number: 2020950043

Published by FutureCycle Press
Athens, Georgia, USA

ISBN 978-1-952593-08-6

For Lewis

Contents

Psalm 63

*⁶ I remember thee upon my bed, and meditate on thee
in the night watches. Because thou hast been my help.*

Night comes by the house—that dull guest with long
sighs—and I settle in silence and wait.
Night is sense, not motion; it's old order:
be still, quiet, swaddled. Die and sleep.
Should I stir, I might notice how night's mine.
The dark is what I give it—breath, moans, hymns.
I'll add what I see, hear beyond the pitch.
My close and blurred hand will edge surfaces,
and I'll toe-feel where feet follow the floor.
I'll watch how night is end and beginning,
and when morning arrives with cardinal
skies—the wren-tint of early—then I'll want
to rise, want to open my singing lips,
to pass through day and into the next night.

Psalm 119

114 Thou art my hiding place and my shield: I hope in thy word.

A child's chore was purpose most personal,
so I studied the ways to use a broom—
the brisk short strokes that spanned the basement steps,
the broad scythe-sweeps that stretched to driveway sides,
the forward push behind parade horses.
I'd read the story about Elijah
and the broom tree, when he hid in shade plants—
crouching, curling dark in his safe sleep.
It was his fortune that desert flowers
have those white blooms and a tropical scent,
leaves for soft rest, bristles to nettle dirt.
So now, in the *tsk, tsk* of a sweeping
task, I train broom straws to a slant—to probe
corners, to check for a safe spot under the bed.

Psalm 78

*15 He clave the rocks in the wilderness, and gave them
drink as out of the great depths.*

I'd want to leave the wilderness.
Surrounded by everything I
needed, I'd still cinch my robe, tie
high my sandals, and let loose my
toes to kick the dust in early morning light.
I'd give up those nights—the pillow
rocks, that hard ground, darkness
the depth and doom of a fathom.
I'd need to remember the wild—
how I'd run my fingers over
the spine-edged acacia.
But I'd never rest easy there;
I'd always itch to move towards
the long reach of smoke, flame of fire.

Psalm 18

28 For thou wilt light my candle: the Lord my God will enlighten my darkness.

Feed upon the light—dine well, chew slowly.
Know the bites are bits of time—natural
light measures—dawn, noon, evening, midnight.
See in the oatmeal dim how the egg cooks
tender in 8 minutes 20 seconds—
the time of light's speed from sun to kitchen.
See how it is no light that makes light real
in that Cape Cod closet where a child plays
among empty arms and Brylcreem collars.
See where light points, when the poet returns
from Italy, imports words about air
that changes illumination, how hard
edges of olive wood become landscape
paintings mixed in linseed oil and beeswax.

Psalm 135

⁷ He causeth the vapors to ascend from the ends of
the earth; he maketh lightnings for the rain, he bringeth
the wind out of his treasuries.

St. Francis says I should travel
tranquil through the world, like rivers.
He wants me to adore breaths spent
in the clouded chill of exhale.
He tells me, be one with vapors
from moving waters. Be fluid,
ride rising and falling splashes.
He's been gilded for a reason,
but when he says abide the drag
on my lungs on cold days, I fail.
I'd rather resist, shrink like old
bodies hiding from death,
follow my instincts. I must know
why I'm caught in river fog.

Psalm 46

10 Be still, and know that I am God.

Be still. Don't forget how the earth shifted—
dinner plates with clean breaks in smashed boxes—
and lands became continents, broken homes.
Be still. Remember. Waters rushed between
the fissures, formed divides, shaped tongues, grew gods,
all holy, right. All lording over all.
Be still and wake early. Walk far. Alone.
But don't dwell on the once-solid land mass
or want it sutured, seamless, with Eden
waters that filled cups, washed hair oils, armpits.
Be, still. Know, still. Endure in the broken.
We did just that when we were uterus
issue, when our hands flailed and tried to cling
to what we were made of. To still be one.

Psalm 136

*⁹ The moon and stars to rule by night: for his mercy
endureth for ever.*

I can't say if we saw Halley's Comet.
I do recall river rafting, riding
white waters—mostly from the rubber raft
floor with a guide who lectured on shifting
paradigms—I'd no idea what he meant.
We had our bad dog and our car lights died
late at night on that thin-laned mountain road.
We must have seen the comet—that's what we
went to do—but I believed then, and now,
that looking at heaven is a study
of distance, questions, not knowing quite where
to look. So I keep glancing up because
I'm certain a raft will float on Class Twos,
the rocks we bounce will only bruise purples.

Psalm 103

*15-16 As for man, his days are as grass: as a flower of
the field, so he flourisheth. For the wind passeth over it,
and it is gone; and the place thereof shall know it
no more.*

The orchid on the porch blossomed today—
the same tropical that languished for two
years with no bloom, just those long, sinewy
blues—vines that looked like old-lady leg veins.
Then, it flowered—soft textures, but petals
that never moved, like mounted butterflies.
The orchid book says to stop watering
right before you think it's enough, which doesn't
help much—I'm missing those instincts.
It's like when I read that deep calls to deep,
am I hearing plinks in pails, rain-barrels?
Is it the echo in a rock quarry?
Is it the call of the orchid that thrives
in low light, stony ground, little water?

Psalm 42

⁷ Deep calleth unto deep at the noise of thy waterspouts:
all thy waves and thy billows are gone over me.

At Anna Ruby Falls, deep calls to deep—
clarity sprays in those waters, in smells
of fragrant and sour, in the prickle
of gnats and shrubs, in the noise of nothing.
It's solemn, like when I'd sit as a child
on the yard swing with my grandmother, pea
pods between her fingers, bowl in her lap.
The fine hairs framing her face were always
combed in sweat, her apron always wrinkled
in damp from washing—corn, hands, floors, work shirts.
Most of the time she'd worry to the child
next to her and wipe her eyes with her sleeve.
She'd say that when her ship came in, we wouldn't
fret anymore—we'd swim in clear waters.

Psalm 107

*9 For he satisfieth the longing soul, and filleth
the hungry soul with goodness.*

We'd hold hands to hear the blessing when I
was a child, not to encircle our faith
in family—it was to keep us from
picking the crust off a fried-chicken leg.
My father would unfold his napkin, fold
his chin in his neck, mumble a one-prayer
sentence so the biscuits wouldn't get cold.
I'd peek, though, through squints and lash filters, watch
heat steam from the beans, rise from the table.
It was so easy then to dine on grace
before the bad toes curled into commas,
before the cat was the voice in response.
Before my middle became gourd hollow
and my gut began to crackle and groan.

Psalm 23

² He maketh me to lie down in green pastures:
he leadeth me beside the still waters.

The funeral Psalm. At my grandmother's
funeral, Pastor Allen recited
it with one arm raised and eyes shut like he
was heading into the deep end, feet first.
At her service, I was the girl with legs
in plaster casts thigh to toe—mourners put
their hands to mouths and said to each other,
That's Rae's child. She had those operations.
An uncle carried me in his arms up
the many-leveled church steps. Leaving, he
toed for footing to descend. We teetered.
Before he steadied, I squeezed fists and eyes.
I was afraid of this plunge, its calm end
in green pastures next to those still waters.

Psalm 45

7 Thou lovest righteousness, and hatest wickedness:
therefore God, thy God, hath anointed thee with the
oil of gladness above thy fellows.

It's odd so many people carry holy oil.
My bad feet slowed me when I tried to run from them.
I wanted the anointers to have credentials—
a license, degree, stigmata tattooed with palm
oil, or myrrh, cassia, tucked into flowing robes.
The ones who trapped me were lay saints, divine toters:
the old aunt with wispy hair and an airy voice,
a college boy with silverfish eyes—small and quick—
the street corner minister who hailed and wailed when
I arched my feet, my back, and high-stepped down the sidewalk.
But the aunt had tried the oil when I was a child—
I recall sniffing my socks for salad dressing—
so I spared the other healers my faith failure.
I knew too well I was on a slippery slope.

Psalm 56

13 For thou hast delivered my soul from death: wilt not thou deliver my feet from falling, that I may walk before God in the light of the living?

A child prays at bedtime: *keep me from falling*
and the prayer becomes a life-long night dream
that begins at the top of the thirteen
risers, eight inches each, and the stair flight
becomes a dream flight that pillows in down
first a small child's scabbed knees, then a woman's
sutured sense of descent from a top step.
She dreams all her adult life of floating
that flight supine—not flying, escaping—
moving like she's harnessed in stunt cables,
with left knee bent, foot poised on the right calf.
She loves those dreams—they soften hard landings.
The woman revels in the ease when she
settles like an angel, ghost, ember dust.

Psalm 30

*² O Lord, my God, I cried unto thee, and thou
hast healed me.*

At six I'd say, *Well, I'm congenital,*
so when my small girl started dragging her
legs through the house, she hobbled me in fear
that I'd passed her my illness, my weakness,
my fading limbs that stood like unfinished
phrases in an awkward conversation.
I wished her skateboard speed and bike hair,
not arches that curled into ball-bearing houses,
not burning feet that slowed failed firewalkers,
not ankles that flopped—socks in a dryer.
But the doctor announced she was healthy,
and my child said she limped to walk like me.
There's no irony here—the doctor erred.
I had indeed given my child my all.

Psalm 73

*2 But as for me, my feet were almost gone; my steps had
well nigh slipped.*

My daughter says I abandoned her to the faith
healer at the flea market, the one who said she
was ninety—it did look like I left her alone—
but I was pushing my child's wheelchair, so she was
between me and the old lady, my girl's legs
plaster-casted like fallen Greek statues, putting
me at a distance from the woman blocking us.
I couldn't run over the old lady when she loomed
forth, commanded with arms stretched for apple plucking,
I'm going to heal your bones. Now rise, get up and walk.
I backed away to clear a path, mumbled that she
couldn't put weight on her feet. It's possible
I may have fled, but it's understood: salvation
is a choice, and I knew my daughter would be fine.

Psalm 116

*15 Precious in the sight of the Lord is the death
of his saints.*

The significance of neighbor Susie
who died at five is that she died at five.
The spring of her dying was notable—
I'd pursed my lips, whistled like a kettle;
counted fear's distance in thunder, lightning.
I learned high and low tones travel downhill.
I'd heard the night air that carried shrill-pitched
child's pain—where it landed flat—fact, not friend.
Within weeks after Susie was gone, I
passed her in age while she lingered uphill—
I waved to her in the moon—but by fall
she was known for her death, not her long braid.
I grew—she didn't—and I soon forgot
the death of a child is not fact, it's grief.

Psalm 122

122 I was glad when they said unto me, Let us go into the house of the Lord.

We'd go, curled in lace anklets and resolve,
to church— twice on Sunday, back on Wednesday.
In summer, we'd march into Bible School,
with high knees and purpose, to the only
morning devotion that I remember.
The solemn minister spoke of sheep bloat—
dense gas trapped, distended, in the stomach—
and how the shepherd punctured the swollen
ovine side, but what escaped exploded.
I forget the analogy. Maybe
we were puffed up—overfed sheep God would
nick, or maybe it was about our pride.
The message matters little—I got stuck
on those bursting bellies in a pasture.

Psalm 144

[1] Blessed be the Lord my strength which teacheth
my hands to war, and my fingers to fight:

Bottle-fed. Baptist-bred. Petticoat-clad.
Georgia-born in the mid-last century.
And Sunday School-raised on Bible Sword Drills
where I lined up straight, back stiff, arms rigid,
to hold the Good Book—tome heft and tomb weight—
to beat other little girls for that cross
on the piano in the church basement.
We'd face and, on command, find the verse first.
We'd sing, pounding notes into loud war chords,
and onward the Christian soldiers would pulse.
And I'd pledge—to the American Flag,
to the Christian Flag—being there for gold stars.
We were holy warriors in shiny
patent leathers in a milk-breath death march.

Psalm 2

*2 Why do the heathen rage and the people imagine
a vain thing?*

Heathen couldn't rage on Sunday mornings
at a grandmother's house when the nasal
chords of stained-glass bluegrass on TV woke
a child, and a preacher hollered, his voice
shrill to reach heaven. He'd clutch his Bible
like a rolled-up newspaper to swat flies,
pestilence, sin. The child loved them—TV
heads of fine-parted men, high-haired women,
the way they clustered before arched windows
of primary colors. She'd sit on her
knees, awed when they leaned to the mic, lifted
throats and palms. Doomed, then saved, in 4/4 time.
She wanted to live in their cloister, raise
her hands high like she was being held up.

Psalm 14

*2 The Lord looked down from heaven upon the children
of men, to see if there were any that did understand,
and seek God.*

I choked air first as a newborn,
then as an upset child wanting,
wanting to be held, wanting my
eyes pressed into muted darkness
against a fine-fabric shoulder.
I gasped air as a young woman,
and as an old, lame woman, too,
always with eyes looking wildly,
head pecking the grist from the grasp—
a chicken bobbing the barnyard.
Here I am, wanting. To be held,
the whole, the holy, the clench
I knew about that first moment
I gasped for air—at the first wail.

Psalm 4

*8 I will both lay me down in peace, and sleep: for thou,
Lord only makest me dwell in safety.*

Journey proud is Southern-say for the nerves
that twist in bedsheets on nights before trips.
It's when travelers awake before wasp-
needled alarms to pack, re-check, foot-tap
with tension, scratch the anxiety itch
that crawled the dark like bedbugs on the skin.
My grandfather didn't suffer *journey
proud*—he tilled, toiled the earth, and loathed the road.
When others went to Table Rock, he stayed
home, settled with his Coke and recliner.
At home, he knew the exchange rate—that when
he turned soil in his garden wood lice crawled
on grit, rolled beyond the loose toss of dirt.
He knew corn planted in spring stalked the fall.

Psalm 1

*3 And he shall be like a tree planted by the rivers
of water, that bringeth forth his fruit in his season;
his leaf also shall not wither; and whatsoever he doeth
shall prosper.*

We go on a Sunday to the old church,
one parent gone in mind, the other weak
in body, though they swap places at will.
It's homecoming—when the Baptists round up
the past or the young who mow lawns, play golf.
My parents sit close, cloaked in habit, hope.
When they slump their round shoulders and chins down,
they both look like they're sleeping—I can't tell.
When they stand, they rock, tremble the hymnal
that neither reads, that sways their gravity.
I hear the breathy vocals of lungs, lips—
musty, empty as hot-water bottles.
They seem content, at home, here in this place
they know—this place on and above the earth.

Psalm 92

¹⁴ They shall still bring forth fruit in old age; they shall
be fat and flourishing.

She'd wake in the nursing home. Every day,
she'd grab the phone, dial the operator.
Her call would go straight to the nurse who'd lie:
This is the bank, how're you today? Always
the old woman would ask, *How's my money?*
The nurse would say, *Your money is safe, Dear!*
Then, even that memory-worry crawled
like a dog under the house. What had gnawed
and pulled a taut leash now curled in moldy earth.
Her wrinkles softened, like she'd found Sunday
dinner cooked and steaming on the table.
And she danced. Her fists unclenched, hands dangled.
She'd laugh, like she'd found vine-ripe tomatoes
ready to drop—red, rain-washed, and sun-warmed.

Psalm 84

*3 Yea, the sparrow hath found a house, and the swallow
a nest for herself.*

The last of the housecoated women are dying.
They'd rise early, snap shapeless cotton over hips
widened by babies; over laps, their metal bowls
of shelled peas; over knees bent to scrub tubs and ears.
They'd cook breakfast seven days a week—eggs, bacon,
biscuits—pack lunches, stand in the door to watch their
sobbing children break switches, switch them right again.
The housecoated women swept stoops of their houses
with vigor, shampooed their children's scalps with their nails,
seldom laughed but yanked their families home-tight
-—like made beds, sashed dresses, and pin-curls. Board solid—
like air-dried laundry washed in scents of grass and trees.
Mostly, those housecoats dangle in Goodwill stores now,
remembering homes—like the children they cradled.

Psalm 88

*8 Thou hast put away mine acquaintance far from me;
thou hast made me an abomination unto them: I am
shut up, and I cannot come forth.*

My old mother picked chicken chunks from the hot soup
with her fingers and pronounced her dementia thoughts
aloud: *My brains are non-active. There's nothing left.*
She spoke like she was reading a fortune cookie,
like she was unfurling a message to amuse.
I wonder why she said "brains," plural. Sometimes she'd
say she was of two minds, or, *I've got one good mind.*
Why didn't she just pick "gone" instead of "non-active,"
why high-brow sounds from a tongue slowing to a halt?
How'd she know that nothing was left—she referenced
a baseline, worded a measure of quantity.
Did she know me, or did she speak to the soup peas?
Was this clarity, and how often did it stir
to plow through her mind like meal moths in the flour?

Psalm 51

8 Make me to hear joy and gladness; that the bones
which thou has broken may rejoice.

David wants joy *and* gladness. I want clarity.
Distinction in translation. Word definitions.
There is a truth in gladness—it's the cataract
eye that refracts grey light, sees insights with aging.
And truth has a stillness—ink on a love letter.
My gladness when my mother said, long after she
forgot me but right before she died, *I'm sorry.*
You're the one who was always there for me.
But joy holds all that's good. Once I watched a toddler
eat a grape—no seeds—she curled soft skin on soft skin
and plopped it in her mouth, sunk a new tooth into
the flesh of what's just right. She laughed and went for more.
There's the true and good—the red tulips I planted
to color one spring. They came back year after year.

Psalm 139

3 Thou compassest my path and my lying down, and art acquainted with all my ways.

A delicate compass. It would have been
my grandmother, gone some 50 years now,
who sent me the cardinals just last summer,
who wanted me to know she was present.
So the birds came—dozens of long stemmed reds,
in three cities. A diva's dressing room.
They'd gather, like old men at the bus stop,
step near the line between awe and worry.
This happened. One knocked on the glass porch door,
again and again butting its bird head,
and I was alarmed there'd be wings, feathers,
bone in red-on-red under the roses.
I missed the message then, but I'm touched now
they came, said, *Be quick. Your mother goes soon.*

Psalm 131

*2 Surely I have behaved and quieted myself, as a child
that is weaned of his mother: my soul is even as a
weaned child.*

It's awkward—I've just buried my mother.
She'd dementia-died long ago, and I'm
swimming in the sea greens, nodding my head,
smiling—a polite mourner—but I'm not
grieving. She's not fighting against currents.
Now, it's just me drifting, legs wandering,
arms opening for sad-eyed embraces—
I'm pivoting, netting regrets, brushing
aside sympathy like kelp in my face.
I'm not tasting my own words in my mouth
on burial day—they're things she would've said,
You're so kind. It's a blessing. She's at peace.
Soon I'll recall who she was—find loss, not
death in the barb—the fishhook in the lip.

Psalm 37

*18 The Lord knoweth the days of the upright: and their
inheritance shall be for ever*

When I bend to him, his stubble scratches
my palm, but his skin is soft, infant-like.
He looks airy—he might drift off towards
his origin—you can tell he goes soon.
I look to see how one of my hands holds
his, the other pincers his jacket sleeve.
I'll have to let go, let him pass—this is
just a single moment in a cold day
when asphalt is stenciled with leaves long gone.
I must let him assume his whole story,
and, looking at the entirety, he will
be a still man rising like the metal
figure in the park on an iron-green stand
where time's patina will burnish his mien.

Psalm 71

¹⁸ Now also when I am old and greyheaded, O God,
forsake me not; until I have shewed thy strength unto
this generation, and thy power to every one that is
to come.

If my father dies today, and I'm not
there, would he have said all he had to say?
Sometimes he'd tell of army days, or his
paper route as a boy, or time at Tech.
He also had a quiet that didn't
matter—we were two who could sit silent.
But just last week he rubbed his chin and asked,
Have l told you how beef jerky is made?
I said we'd save that for another time,
for a day when we would shave thin pieces
of idle wag, season chatter with salt,
chew on the lean fat of meaningless talk.
Still, I should have that exchange now, savor
sounds of words in my mouth that I can taste.

Psalm 104

32 He looketh on the earth, and it trembleth.

When my mother died, I ordered up order—
washed the car, cut and colored, dry-cleaned the dress.
Months later, my father followed my mother
to the root cellar, and I shampooed, spit-washed
a spot off my sleeve, and drove fast to the grave-
yard so wind would scatter dust from the four-door.
She went and I was presenting to old, new,
higher orders—to swift sucks—like kitchen sink
eddies. Like storm water rushing the downspouts,
drowning flower bulbs. Like brown slush in April.
My father went, but I'd learned I had nothing
to gain with Sunday clothes, shiny nails, plucked brows.
I'd studied the quick—saw I need only know
how sleep-tight eyes block the dark but not the dreams.

Psalm 33

2 Praise the Lord with harp: sing unto him with the psaltery and an instrument of ten strings.

Those who've gone before come when the music
starts-—Opal, Rae, Pat—the chords summon them
to my pew, like organs have call buttons
to my dead. And, they don't care what they hear:
Widor's *Toccata,* Fauré's *Requiem,*
the solo in *Royal David's City,*
even movie-made *Gabriel's Oboe.*
Only music brings them to me—not scents
of magnolia blooms with brown-edged bruises.
Not the crackled crust of new-baked pound cake.
Not the coffee taste of a day-long pot.
I know where to find them, and more join us
all the time now—just filling up that brown bench—
bodies and beats all mixed up in marked time.

Psalm 150

*3 Praise him with the sound of the trumpet: praise him
with the psaltery and harp.*

I listened to Leonard Cohen all day
on the Wednesday after the election.
The next day Leonard Cohen fell and died.
It was hard to mourn Cohen with Cohen.
Overkill of the senses. Dye swallows
that found the porous weak spots and drowned them.
A drone that erased the path and target.
The stage lights that blinded the audience.
That was the week I couldn't find either
the holy or the broken chords, the week
it all went wrong, but I was left with head hums
of the hallelujah. Soft sounds that moved
my fingers into braille beats that became
sad songs. Music without lyrics or notes.

Psalm 91

6 Nor for the pestilence that walketh in darkness;
nor for the destruction that wasteth at noonday.

I bought potting soil so alive fruit flies
swarmed, kissed, and licked my cheeks like Coke bubbles.
I wanted to nurture the baby's tears,
bleeding hearts, peace plants—but the flies dipped their
bodies into cursive air ink and wrote,
You've come to the age where you cannot see.
That's not so, I argued, I have great skill—
I read fists, hunched shoulders, eyes that shoot rooms
to an eye—like a rubber band on thumb
and index—the release, the double sting.
I've always relied on pattern—people
have meter and syllables have rhythm.
The flies nagged, nettled, said—*The minute you*
think you know, you're just carrion with flies.

Psalm 50

¹⁰ For every beast of the forest is mine, and the cattle upon a thousand hills.

There could be a reason my cat shows grace.
A woman from the church brought her to me.
She roves the house, bestowing redemption.
The frayed fabric mouse she leaves on my bed—
it's her sermon on the Beatitudes.
The fern fronds she plucks, places in my shoe—
she's a church lady arranging flowers.
She's grateful— those teeth will always be gone,
but her street wounds healed. Still, she hides, cloisters.
The house painters called me a crazy cat
lady with an imaginary cat.
They never see her, but I do. She moves
room-to-room with assurance, connection.
She kneels, knowing, in the greatest repose.

Psalm 36

6 Thy righteousness is like the great mountains; thy judgments are a great deep: O Lord, thou preservest man and beast.

Windows shine high from the cabin
built on one side of a steep hill.
The gorge is deep but the valley
isn't wide, and I want to stretch
to brush ferns on the hill across.
I have my ways. Every day I
do the same thing—pour my coffee,
stare at curved earth that's out of reach.
I drink only from one side, hold
the cup with both hands—an offering.
I study this hill—try to grasp
how it happened, how it's hollowed,
how time, twigs run with rainwater
down the valley, on that deer trail.

Psalm 142

*¹ I cried unto the Lord with my voice; with my voice
unto the Lord did I make my supplication.*

I should watch myself, note my sequences
of sadness—how I respond in habit
when I steer around the driveway pot hole.
Reflex first curls me smaller—a rain frog.
Sometimes I groan—the old dog in the shed.
Or I'll wonder why it must be this way—
yet another cow in another field
with a stockyard at the pasture's end.
Then I get humble, honest, eyeball earth
and scratch dirt—a barnyard chicken—before
I appeal, make that short-flapped poultry flight.
And when good comes, I'm the somber peahen,
a starched marcher, braided in full dress
on parade, strutting the onus of love.

Psalm 147

16 He giveth snow like wool: he scattereth the hoarfrost like ashes.

It's January in Georgia, that sometimes time
when pine trees snap and black ice saran-wraps the roads.
I get winter-brained. My cold nose chills sinuses.
My eyes cataract in the sun's limited days.
My sentences are first lines and nothing follows—
they're the rows between spent stalks in corn fields.
My words are stanza breaks, white space between chapters.
The short notes I jot down—ancient hieroglyphics
without history, that say *Only this, Only now.*
And ideas. They're lame iambs, calloused by tight
boots that scramble and stumble on a bleak hardscape.
It's January in Georgia, when my head can't
sense, can't face forward or backward, or find pattern
in a turn of words, in this rotation of earth.

Psalm 24

[8] Who is this King of glory? The Lord strong and mighty, the Lord mighty in battle.

Our starter house was the ranch for the new
marriage, wet baby, the trench in the back,
in woods to the mill where soldiers rutted.
Where war would rest at night on pine needles
and men would whisper of willful horses,
a fish that got away, a girl that didn't.
They would hunch, wait, and swat mosquitoes, taste
dry-mouth, fight tremors, and notice bullets
took liberty with language, how the holes
opened not with the clarity of day—
they were pulpy wonders. May's azaleas.
Their wounds looked like the gully muscadines—
purple flesh, drooping globs that eased from meat
in the swale, split ripe in the blade of sun.

Psalm 25

⁴ Show me thy ways, O lord; teach me thy paths.

The right angle in the road where I live
was once called Dead Man's Corner. No one says
that now—it's just Jesus Junction, where three
churches spire over a curve and several
times each month, plus holidays, drivers slam
into a wall at the turn in the road.
Cars hit only at night—traffic slows risk—
that's when speed shape-shifts moments into wrecks—
tires and skulls into bricks spined with rebar.
For years, right when the wall collapses, they
call the brick layer to say *come back, fix
it again.* The fact is, nothing stops the cars—
bodies are going to follow their heads.
They think they know where the road should take them.

Psalm 68

*21 But God shall wound the head of his enemies,
and the hairy scalp of such an one as goeth on still in
his trespasses.*

I

I study how to project my power:
First, keep my limbs away from my body.
Then, I mustn't let my fingers worry
with the loose button thread on the raincoat.
Also, I note to never cross my arms
over my chest—it looks like I'm shielding
my organs from shrapnel. And if I grab
my wrists, I look like a kid stretching
the shirt sleeves I've outgrown, hiding skin.
And forget about ever taking one
finger to the frayed cuticle at hand,
or, God forbid, scissor it with my teeth.
Thus, I can never touch my face or twirl
my hair into the fray of submission.

Psalm 68

21 But God shall wound the head of his enemies,
and the hairy scalp of such an one as goeth on still in
his trespasses.

II

I think of shape-shifters who shrink girth, breadth,
reduce height with a breath and a repose.
Contortionists don't coil to slither off.
Horned lizards flattened on rocks don't cower.
Head down, eyes-up stance? That's *not* to demur.
I know for a fact it's to prevail, move.
Watch the ground and I spot the rotten wood
in the swinging bulb on the cellar steps.
I shade my face—better that way to catch
a quick glance in an eclipsed look—and I'm
the cornea that spots the gaseous
corona, the dark knell. It's easier
to watch those unaware of witness—it's
the underestimated's advantage.

Psalm 35

22 This thou hast seen, O Lord: keep not silence:
O Lord, be not far from me.

I'm the sum of all my losses—
people who died, left me alone.
Those who clipped ties like loose threads,
The ones I lost who still linger—
wrist waves, nods at funerals.
I include the loss of nothing:
the long silences in short chats,
the poems that never get written.
Memories, hair, sleep, muscle mass.
These losses are a sculptor's marble
dust—they're gone, but they cling to cuffs.
I'm the sum of all my losses—
spaces that fill, the green moss spread
on a stony and cracked walkway.

Psalm 109

22 For I am poor and needy, and my heart is wounded within me.

I cannot lament the tyranny of the weak,
the wide-eyed runt mewling, drooling in the litter,
the one that whines complaints like a tired stump preacher.
And I can't rue the tyranny of the wounded,
especially the messy—sores, sour odors—
I've learned to flinch, narrow the eyes, mouth and just tend—
I gag when I hold the head of one who retches.
Nor can I shirk the tyranny of selflessness,
saintly ones that corner, command, in virtue voice.
And for sure I won't ever flee the tyranny
of piety—that values metric. That endless
metronome, clocking demands on quiet moments.
I watch. Smother flames of dominion in silence.

Psalm 27

*5 For in time of trouble he shall hide me in his pavilion;
in the secret of his tabernacle shall he hide me.*

I wonder if Jesus had place cards at the Last
Supper because they'd had that talk about sitting
on the left, the right, above the salt or below.
Or did they just drop where they last sat: into their
habit, their familiar? One time, I slumped near
the pulpit early, needing words, music, quiet.
A man loomed over me, the oak arm of the church
pew the divide from six-two, heavy-set with feet
apart, fists on hips, and back straight. His words menaced:
You're in my seat. I didn't move but never knelt there
again since he found faith in row five, inside aisle.
It was his place. His order. I sat in the back
but I lacked surety of habit and a view
of the water stain of Mary on the ceiling.

Psalm 55

⁶ And I said, Oh that I had wings like a dove! for then would I fly away, and be at rest.

I'll call upon God; the Lord shall save me.
I fidget with those words like they're rosary
beads, skin tags on the neck, straws in soda.
They're words that seldom convey what I want.
They're urgent-care words, antiseptics to
heal infections rooted deep—like gangrene—
bone-coated and skin-tinged. Forced removals.
I'd rather the words said *Save me from me*
when I believe everything I think.
Like when I never learned to be alpha
to a dog because I couldn't crate it
or when I thought the old homeless woman
in front of my house needed my blanket.
When I thought words were just for ears and books.

Psalm 123

*² …so our eyes wait upon the Lord our God, until that
he have mercy upon us.*

It's a year since my father died—
I measure grief in pajama
days that replace tissue for tears.
He isn't the loss—it wouldn't
be right to want a riled old man
to linger in a cracked-leather
recliner in cracked-leather skin.
I miss most the mundane message—
It's too cold. I'm craving peaches.
When one would speak, the other would nod
at mindless words not meant to last.
So I'm shuffling slippers into
absence—the pulled tooth, the clipped nail
that's of the body, not the body.

Psalm 118

6 The Lord is on my side; I will not fear: what can man do unto me?

Animals know fear. They *show* fear.
A cat burrows beneath pillows,
dog ribs rattle in thundered dread.
The psalmist says, *Do not fear.*
But I worry, work fear's frayed wires.
I might splay my hand over mouth,
a mouth rounded into the *o* of no.
Because I've tasted rockslide mud.
Fingered the milky, cool maggots
that dine on natural order.
So I hold that tension—is, was,
might be—and rinse it in promise.
But what my head knows, my breath fails
to reason—I live hand-to-mouth.

Psalm 140

I cobble—an editor at deadline—
Psalm 140 to Sonnet 140.
God, hear the voice of my supplications.
Lest sorrow lend me words, and words express,
gurgle, flow with bubbles, like deep-cut wounds.
Lest all my words are lamentations, old
parchment ink uplifted in dark scroll script.
Lest I sleep-speak the sorrow-words easy
to utter, waiting to choke and smother.
I'd like to know another language with
words that won't disappoint the sentences.
Then, I'd crack—but wouldn't break—a book's spine
to fill uncut journals with leather-bound
gladness, in the pulp promise of a pine.

Psalm 121

1 I will lift up mine eyes unto the hills, from whence cometh my help.

Nothing has changed: mountain laurel still
fences the narrow path, still a road
cracked, oiled by years and slow-climbs uphill.
Even the midday light's not turned: old
woods remain drab, cloaked in robes, monk-brown.
It's been fifty years. The lake's a wrought
tint of green; that splintered dock's now grown
deep into my finger—an age spot.
Here I braided calm like macramé.
This was church—apse, nave, sanctuary—
when I'd bring a grey trunk stuffed with stray
jabs. Shrill voices that start close, carry.
I'll stay. Days are airy on this ridge.
All's well and this road was—is—a bridge.

Acknowledgments

Allegro: "Psalm 50"
America: The Jesuit Review: "Psalm 103"
Christian Century: "Psalm 1," "Psalm 140"
Ink & Letters: "Psalm 23," "Psalm 73"
Psaltry & Lyre: "Psalm 119," "Psalm 55"
Snapdragon: "Psalm 37"
Sojourners: "Psalm 46"
The Penwood Review: "Psalm 51," "Psalm 63"

The italicized Psalms are taken from the King James version of the Bible.

About FutureCycle Press

FutureCycle Press is dedicated to publishing lasting English-language poetry in both print-on-demand and Kindle formats. Founded in 2007 by long-time independent editor/publishers and partners Diane Kistner and Robert S. King, the press incorporated as a nonprofit in 2012. A number of our editors are distinguished poets and writers in their own right, and we have been actively involved in the small press movement going back to the early seventies.

We award the FutureCycle Poetry Book Prize and honorarium annually for the best full-length volume of poetry we published that year. Introduced in 2013, proceeds from our Good Works projects are donated to charity. Our Selected Poems series highlights contemporary poets with a substantial body of work to their credit; with this series we strive to resurrect work that has had limited distribution and is now out of print.

We are dedicated to giving all of the authors we publish the care their work deserves, offering a catalog of the most diverse and distinguished work possible, and paying forward any earnings to fund more great books. All of our books are kept "alive" and available unless and until an author requests a title be taken out of print.

We've learned a few things about independent publishing over the years. We've also evolved a unique and resilient publishing model that allows us to focus mainly on vetting and preserving for posterity poetry collections of exceptional quality without becoming overwhelmed with bookkeeping and mailing, fundraising activities, or taxing editorial and production "bubbles." To find out more about what we are doing, come see us at www.futurecycle.org.

The FutureCycle Poetry Book Prize

All full-length poetry books published by FutureCycle Press in a given calendar year are considered for the annual FutureCycle Poetry Book Prize. This allows us to consider each submission on its own merits, outside of the context of a traditional contest. Too, the judges see the finished book, which will have benefitted from the beautiful book design and strong editorial gloss we are famous for.

The book ranked the best in judging is announced as the prize-winner in the subsequent year. There is no fixed monetary award; instead, the winning poet receives an honorarium of 20% of the total net royalties from all poetry books and chapbooks the press sold online in the year the winning book was published. The winner is also accorded the honor of being on the panel of judges for the next year's competition; all judges receive copies of all contending books to keep for their personal library.

www.ingramcontent.com/pod-product-compliance
Lightning Source LLC
Chambersburg PA
CBHW070013100426
42741CB00012B/3226